The Blue Fold

The
Blue
Fold

Explorations at Loggerhead Key
Dry Tortugas National Park

Matthew & Julie Chase-Daniel

 Axle Contemporary Press, Santa Fe, New Mexico

This book is published on the occasion of the 2018 exhibition, *The Blue Fold*, organized by the National Parks Arts Foundation, at the Eco-Discovery Center in Key West, Florida. The Center is sponsored and operated by Florida Keys National Marine Sanctuary, the National Oceanic and Atmospheric Administration (NOAA), the South Florida Water Management District, Everglades and Dry Tortugas National Parks, and the National Wildlife Refuges of the Florida Keys.

Published by
Axle Contemporary Press
P.O. Box 22095
Santa Fe, NM 87502

ISBN 978-0-9963991-4-2

CONTENTS

PREFACE

In 2017, Matthew and Julie Chase-Daniel were awarded a residency on Loggerhead Key by the National Parks Arts Foundation. The small island is 70 miles west of Key West, Florida, 80 miles north of Havana, Cuba, and one of seven islands in the Dry Tortugas National Park. The park is home to extensive protected marine habitat and healthy coral reefs. Loggerhead Key houses a decommissioned brick lighthouse built in 1858, a small bunkhouse, a 1926 brick Light Keeper's cottage, and a boathouse now falling into the sea. Power is produced by photovoltaic panels and water by a reverse-osmosis desalination system. The island has no telephone, cell phone or internet service. The month-long arts residency provides uninterrupted time to work and immersion in a natural environment free from many of the distractions of twenty-first century life.

The artists arrived on September 1, but were evacuated less than a week later due to the impending arrival of Hurricane Irma. In the largest mass evacuation in the U.S., they fled with millions as much of south Florida came under mandatory evacuation orders. They spent a week in central Florida at a Holiday Inn in Lady Lake while the hurricane arrived and passed through the area. When the roadways were reopened, they relocated to Miami Beach to explore the effects of the hurricane while waiting to learn if they could go back to the Dry Tortugas. On September 20, they returned to Loggerhead Key, and remained there, alone and uninterrupted until October 10, cleaning up palm fronds and broken glass, walking the island, getting to know the birds and crabs, making photographs, reading, and writing.

INTRODUCTION

The isolation of the island creates a unique rhythm of life, and its dryness, a stark beauty. There are no rocks here, no mosquitoes, no hills, no springs or streams, and no large land animals, except the two of us. We walk the island several times each day. Soon, we feel a sense of intimacy with what is here. When a flock of migratory birds stops in, we notice them, and they notice us. There is little cover, no anonymity.

One day a flock of six cattle egrets lands. They patrol the lawn and the shallows, looking for food. Each time we circle the island we see them all, wherever they are. We learn their struggles, their habits, the way they move when they are happy, sad, or frightened. One by one, the egrets are stalked, killed, and eaten by the newly arrived peregrine falcons. We mourn their loss when we discover their carcasses, and nonetheless delight in the boldness of the peregrines. Such affinity is due in part to the diminutive size of the island. Small as it is, those of us with a stake in the land are all drawn into relationship as we go about the business of our days.

We brought the folding butterfly chair that has traveled everywhere with us for years, and set it up on the porch: Julie's portable writing studio. By day, she takes notes, books and papers cascading around her feet, binoculars at hand. At night she slips out to work, writing until the first streaks of dawn begin to flicker in the sky. Now and then I waken and see her silhouette, wings up, the light from her headlamp like a third eye shining in the dark.

Twice each day the tide rises, scrubs the beach, and deposits fresh treasure and debris. I begin to make small collections and bring them to the house. I find all the conch shells, all the sea urchin shells. I discover richness in the variation of each thing, rather than in the diversity of many things, become fascinated with the scarcity here, how it serves as a frame, illuminating each thing as a representative of its kind.

I make a temporary natural-light studio near the house, using bed sheets and typing paper and buckets. I move it and adjust it as the light changes throughout each day or as the wind and rain come and go. The whiteness and simplicity of the photos is the brightness of the sun, the isolation of the island, the bleached coral sand, the flat landscape.

We live like this for a month, enfolded in the blue of sky and sea, perched on the shifting shoals in a small hollow between ocean swells, searching out perspectives of Loggerhead Key and its guests. At times the island feels likes an extension of us, at others, we feel like an extension of it. As temporary caretakers, we wonder who is taking care of whom.

Our title, *The Blue Fold*, is taken from Julie's poem exploring the perspective of the island itself. Indeed, we hazard multiple views here, folding them into one another, exploring how all perspectives are generative and always-already unfolding from within, even as they are situated and interdependent. Far from discovering the end of the earth, the distant horizon where ocean meets sky is where we caught a line and leapt into the *origami cosmos*, to see what we could see.

The Blue Fold

2   *Sea Urchins*   30 × 30 inches, archival pigment print, 2017

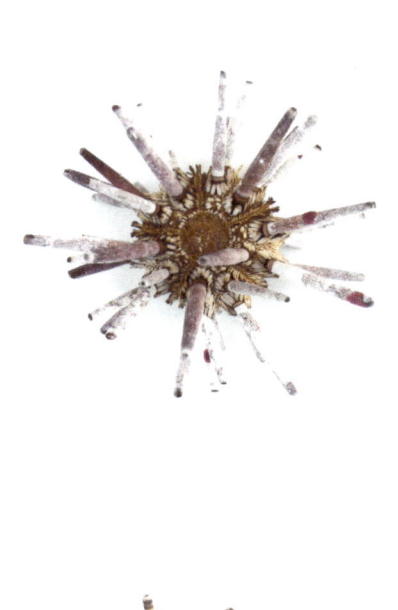
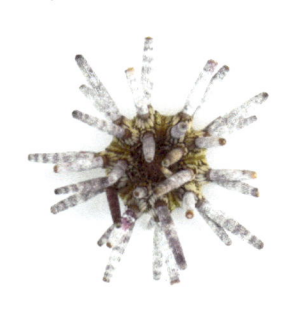
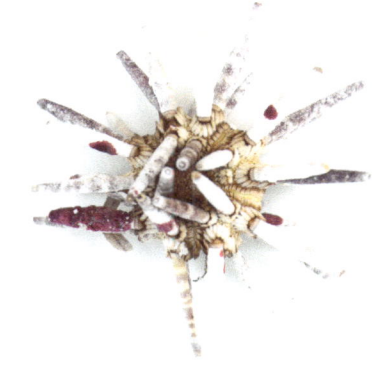
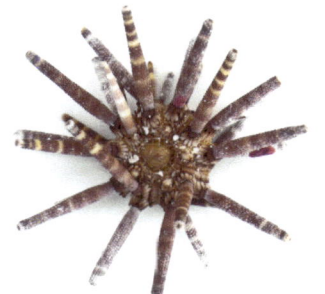
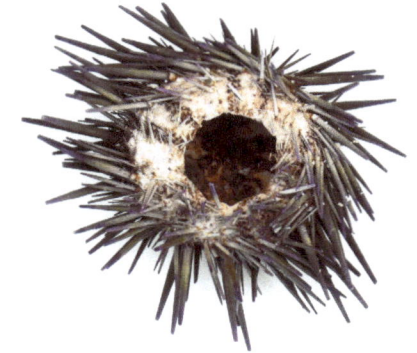
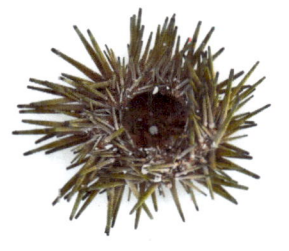
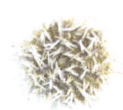
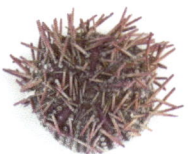
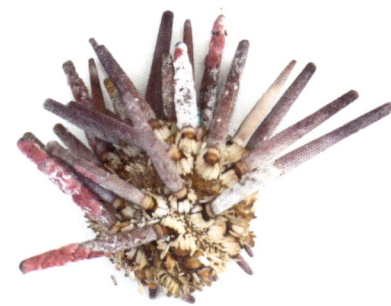

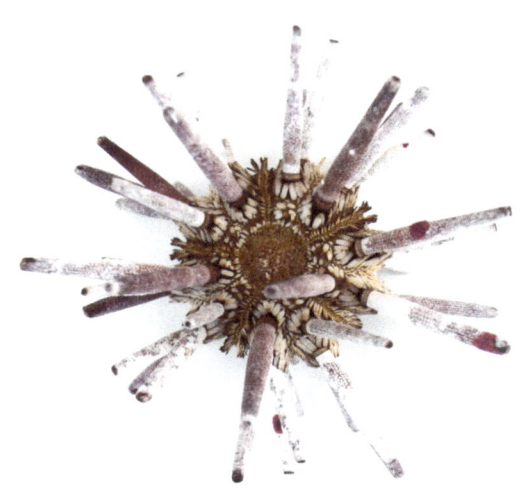

4   *Sea Urchins* (detail)

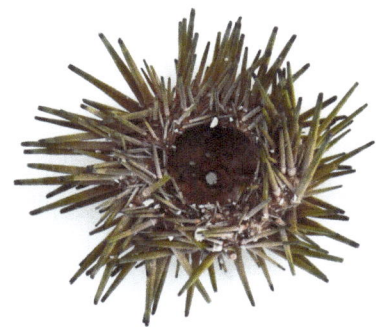

SPIRA MIRABILIS

Salvaged seashell,
home to hermit crab,
Tortugas Gyre
cyclone
limpet
the lighthouse stair
spider's web
milky way
this mortal coil
my path,
labyrinthine,
his green thread,
spooling out,
our cocoon.

8   *Hermit Crabs*   30 × 30 inches, archival pigment print, 2017

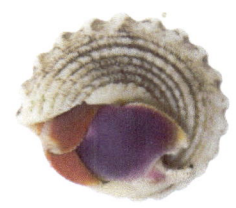
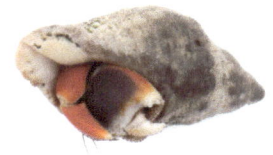
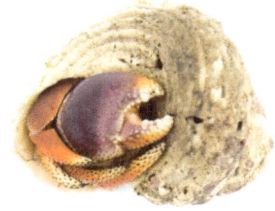
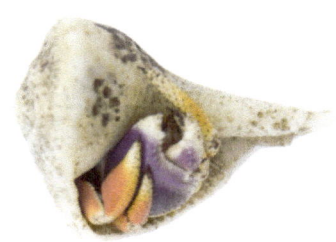
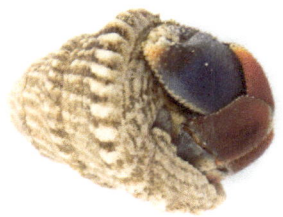
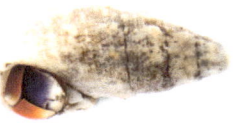
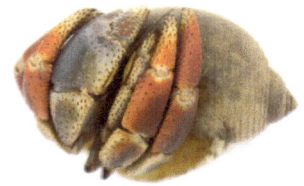
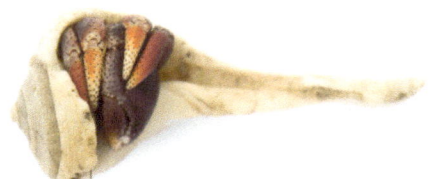
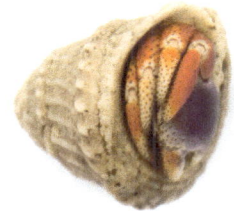

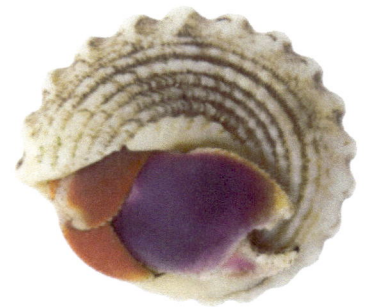

10   *Hermit Crabs* (detail)

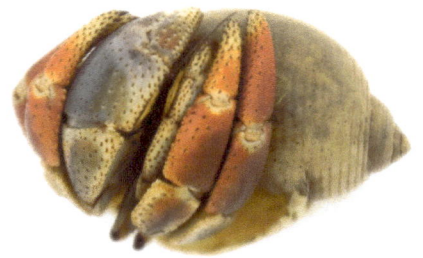

RARE

Spending prolonged time in a spare environment and away from the distractions of our normal lives, our focus intensifies. Looking closely, the broad reaches of white sand are made of countless forms and muted colors. The small forms we find there contain miniature versions of the shells and corals we see lying large above the high tide line. We find a hermit crab, the size of a mayfly, living in a spiral shell the size of the head of a pin. Days before, we had come across the storm-tossed carcass of a giant hermit crab the size of a lobster, inside a conch shell. We had never before seen one so small, nor one so large.

With the geographic and environmental range of the island being so restricted, we see that there are few examples of anything: two sea grape bushes, six cattle egrets, seven houseflies. And colors are restricted. Orange appears rarely, in a tiny seashell, the wing of a redstart fluttering into the brush, the cambium of a broken bay cedar, the claw of a crab. The orange flashes like a fleeting fire. It is nowhere else but briefly in the western sky at sunset on the stormy days.

14   *Tiny Shells*   30 × 30 inches, archival pigment print, 2017

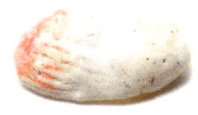
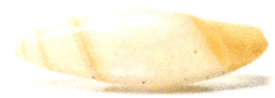
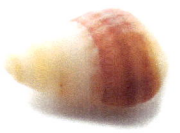
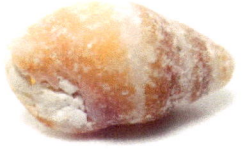
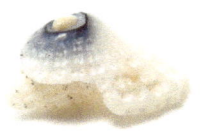
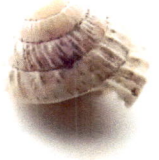
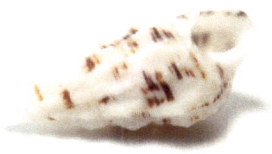
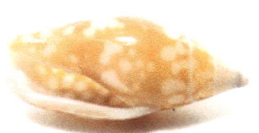
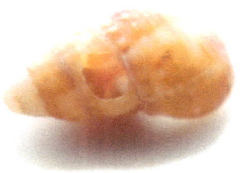

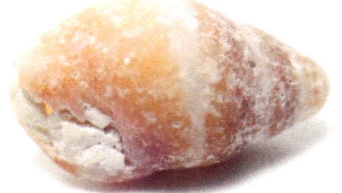

16   *Tiny Shells* (detail)

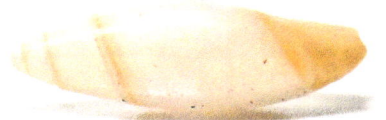

Tiny Shells (detail)   17

YOU WANT TO TELL THEM THINGS

So you reach with your grass,
stroking their feet, you say
this is a long story,
the unfolding of it
or its end
is up to you.
Listen.
Listen, you say,
while they look and look.
Casting your gentle touch
to the wind
you drive them away
by hurricane
you fling your sand
from one side to the other
you pull the fruit from the trees
scorch every leaf
rip out the lilies.
You raise the tide
suck them in a little too deep.
Again and again
you pull down the dock
but they return nonetheless
their looking never stops.
You summon the clouds
you shower them
you tear at their clothes.

The air is thick with your voice
guttural, howling,
whistling, you call in the raptors to
feast on the songbirds, a ritual
of carnage. By full moon
at perigee you hammer
all night, glaring
you stoke the sun
burn their round faces.
Eventually they go, melting
back into their blue fold,
the way of all the others.
You don't know if they
learned your language or if
they could even hear you.
On to the next guests,
you'll never hear them
say: our island
is a shuddering microcosm,
speaking for the earth,
you'll never see this,
the fruit of
all that looking,
with its hopeful stone,
what's come of them
now, in the flesh
after you.

20   *Immature Coconuts*   30 × 30 inches, archival pigment print, 2017

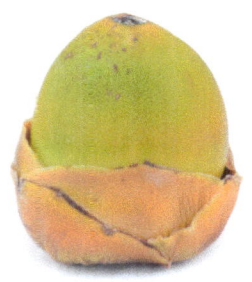
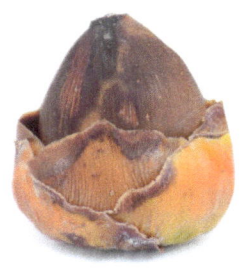
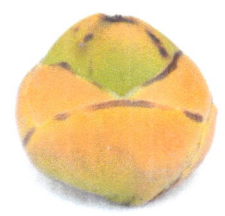
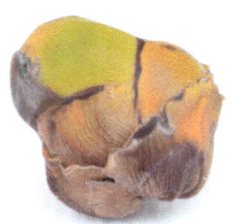
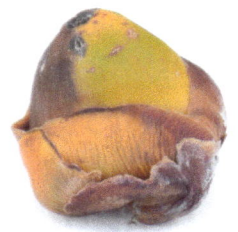
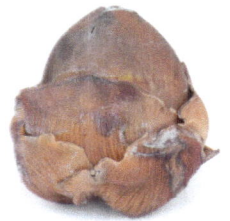
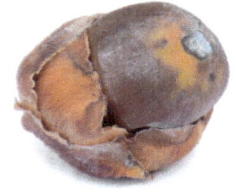
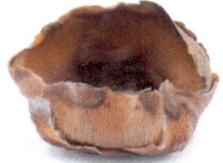
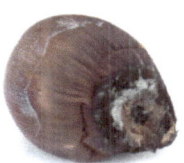

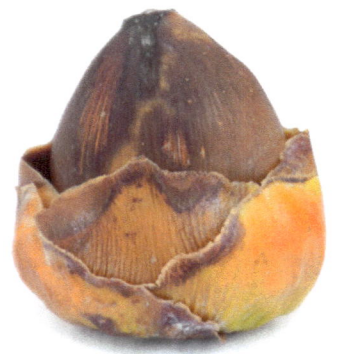

Immature Coconuts (detail)

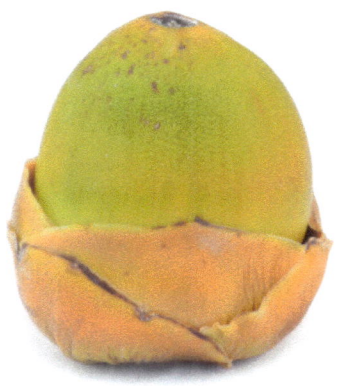

Immature Coconuts (detail)   23

NO ISLAND IS AN ISLAND, EVACUATION REPORT

Driving all night under a thickening sky, we are at the front of a wave of evacuees leaving Key West ahead of Hurricane Irma. The roads are quiet, our headlights first in a sporadic line behind us. Gas is available everywhere. Still, we take only a little at a time whenever we stop, learning as we go how to be runners. Our thinking is oddly muddled, we know only that we have to leave, that we can't get home, and that if possible we want to get back to the island when it's over. Our residency has changed shape, and we've decided to follow it where it leads.

In Lady Lake, a retiree community in central Florida, we find the plaza booming with merrymakers who have all arrived by golf cart from nearby housing tracts quaintly called villages. Red Rum Irmas are flowing freely, and a local band is belting out *Purple Haze* from the gazebo while a fountain bubbles nearby amid the faux ruins of a Spanish mission. It's a deluge, and we sink into it hesitantly, guests in an America we've read about but never seen up close. We are not as out of place as we feel – another thing to think about – but later, after a soft meal at the corner cafe. Precious bubble collapsing, we hunker down and learn that waiting out a catastrophic storm is an art in itself, expressed in countless small acts of kindness, companionship, and generosity.

We awaken to flooding, power outages, downed trees, blocked roads, curfews, and gas shortages after Irma passes through at over one hundred miles per hour. News from the worst hit areas begins to filter in, humanitarian relief efforts begin immediately. We sign up to assist, but are not called. We wonder, again, what we are doing here, our minds blurry with the unfamiliar. Gradually we regain our sense of purpose, remember who we are: park service volunteers, artists who came here specifically in order to surrender to the unfamiliar in nature and make something of it, an offering, for an increasingly disconnected world.

In support of our nation's public lands, Theodore Roosevelt once said "We have fallen heirs to the most glorious heritage a people ever received, and each one must do his part if we wish to show that the nation is worthy of its good fortune." While we wait to learn how and if we can help with the natural resource recovery efforts in the Dry Tortugas, and whether we will be able to resume our residency on the island, we decide to focus our attention on nearby state and national parks. We discover they are all closed, crisscrossed with broken electrical poles and wires, trees and debris. Tired and discouraged park rangers tell us they don't know when they will be able to reopen, even they are restricted in what they can do. Everyone, it seems, is at least slightly adrift, like us, their parts difficult to discern in the wake of Irma.

As soon as the road opens, we head back down the peninsula to Miami Beach, where friends have kindly offered us a place to stay. When we arrive, we begin assessing what the storm has wrought, damage and beauty: unfamiliar tropical trees, flowers, and fruits spread around on the street, to be seen in an intimacy in their deaths that was distant in their lives. But as we walk the streets, we are witness to a rising frenetic collective urge to quickly trim and haul and sweep. That energy is everywhere, a deep-set need to return to normal, to put the storm and all its fear and dread in the past. By the third day, most of the downed trees have been chopped up and hauled away, wind-blown shrubbery has been straightened or removed, and street signs crumpled to the ground have been replaced.

The beach here is endangered, threatened by extreme erosion, as are all the beaches up and down the Florida coast. There is still a beach in Miami Beach, but today it is a graveyard. Mounds of sea grass, where turtles shelter as hatchlings in the teeming marine equivalent of a tropical rain forest, have been wrenched from the sea floor and are dying in thick beds at the tide line. Jellyfish, sponges, and coral wash up with every small wave. Much of the sand that was placed here last year has withdrawn. Soon, no doubt, the efforts to rescue the beach will resume, with boats sucking up new sand from the deep sea floor and trucks depositing up to 300,000 tons from inland sand mines. In the meantime, the concrete paths are already filling again with spandex joggers and bikinied revelers, hungover college students are coffeeing up at early morning beachside cafes after long nights at the club, while the children of oligarchs flaunt their boob jobs, diamonds, and Maseratis, spending money like water.

Momentarily subdued by Hurricane Irma, the island returns quickly to hawking itself to the highest bidder in the seaside bars, where

North, South, and Central American tourists banter in rapid and diverse languages, food and drink is for the rich, and the beach, bars, and restaurants are home to the beautiful. It's a sybaritic deluge of alcohol and tits and ass, a crowded, dripping, humid representation of humanity's beauty, foolishness, and endless consumption. Seeking refuge, we spend a day walking the length of Key Biscayne. Beginning where Miami Beach ends, this bay marks one end of the Florida Keys National Marine Sanctuary, which encompasses the southern reach of Florida and stretches all the way out to the Dry Tortugas.

Loggerhead Key and Miami Beach come into perspective as bookends, of our residency and of the reef, of nature and culture. Their stories could not be more different. When Juan Ponce de Leon stopped in the Dry Tortugas in 1562, there were eleven islands, and those all were still extant in the eighteenth century. Now they number only seven, four having been swept away by the sea in the interim. When, inevitably, Loggerhead Key erodes back into the ocean, no one will attempt to stop that process. It is clear that nothing could be done. Despite its old lighthouse and historic ruins of the Carnegie marine research lab, Loggerhead is a natural place. No one who steps here could be fooled that this place isn't ephemeral and exists grace to chance and vagaries of climate and current which all are now changing with increasing pace.

Miami Beach was the same, only moments ago in geologic time. It too is only sand and porous limestone, and as sea levels rise, this island city will inexorably disappear. But this isn't seen or accepted. Something will be done, a solution will be found, is the common refrain. Streets are being raised and massive drains and pumps installed, while architect superstars design new towers and construction crews are hard at work, even just days after the hurricane. The mangroves are long gone from the inland shore, replaced by concrete seawalls and granite riprap. At this writing, the language and science of climate change and global warming have been banned from public policy discussions, a governmental barricade of denial that keeps the money flowing. How long any of these walls will hold is anyone's guess.

Our efforts to observe and draw meaning from untrammeled nature can only be successful to the extent we can find it, whether in the Dry Tortugas or anywhere along our evacuation route. No island is an island, we've discovered, an inversion of John Donne's *17th Meditation on Emergent Occasions*. From Loggerhead Key with its monuments, resident interns, fellow volunteers, and day visitors, to central Florida, and now in Miami Beach, humanity dominates the landscape everywhere. Now, as some measure of normal life resumes in much of Florida, and damage assessments come in from the Everglades and Dry Tortugas, we wait to learn if and when we might get back to the island. Immersed in this emergent occasion that is Hurricane Irma, we venture out for photos of the small and intimate fragile points of nature and change wherever we may find them.

Coconut Spathes   30 × 30 inches, archival pigment print, 2017

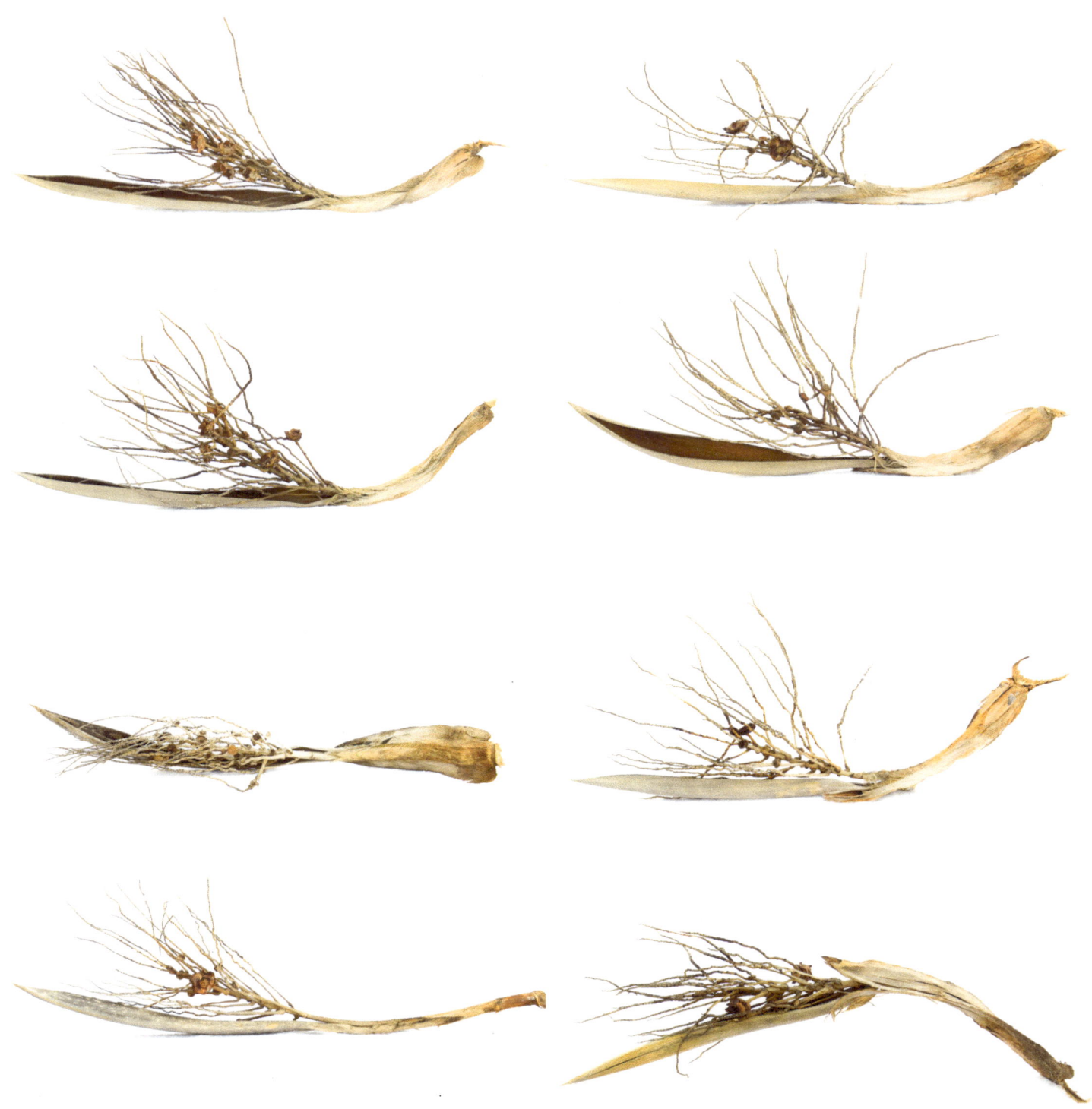

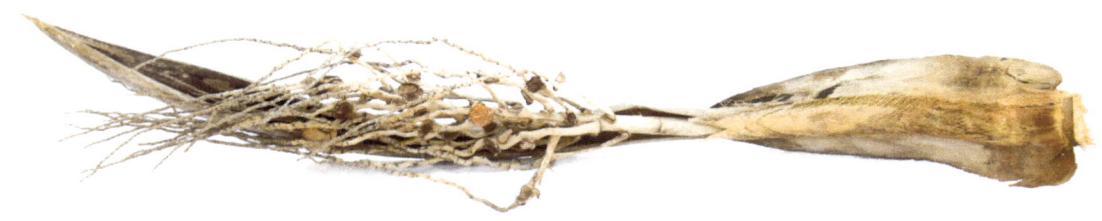

Coconut Spathes (detail)

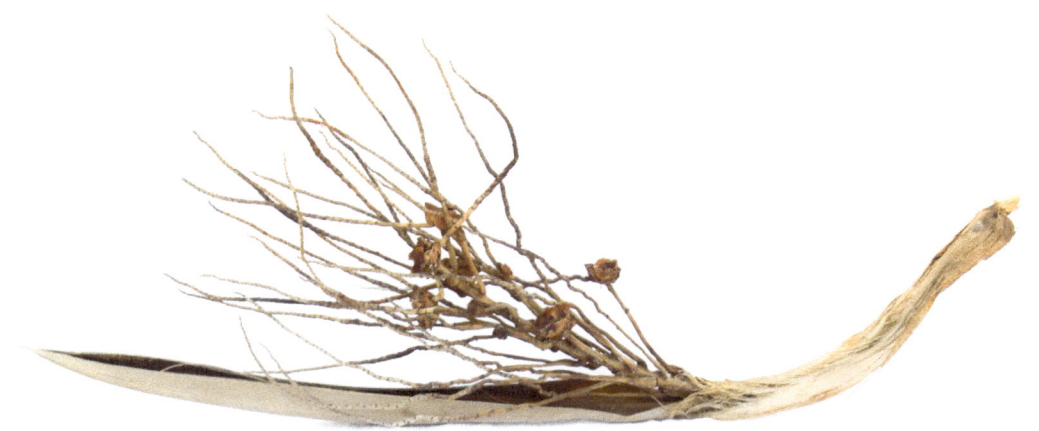

Coconut Spathes (detail)   33

PRESERVATION

In death the lilies
lie down
like long-necked egrets,
graceful in their green
bed of infinitely
long duration,
but the birds
we find
look like exhausted
angels crashed to earth,
simply unable
to carry on
for even one more
blessed second.

We see traces of a turtle,
tracks leading to her
wide V-bottomed nest
certain to be full,
soft white eggs
deep down, a deposit
safe, at least for now
and triumphant
in the tattered landscape.
My thoughts turn

toward the little kid
in the Haggadah
who asks every year
what does all this
have to do with me?

None of us imagines
we are that wicked
one, certainly not I,
who must learn
again and again
we are all connected,
no boundary,
one and the same.

If you know the story,
you know this, and that
it's about survival.
And how it is in
the telling
each year that we re-
member the world,
return to the fold over
and over, across
the distance of our questions.

Coconut Stems   30 × 30 inches, archival pigment print, 2017

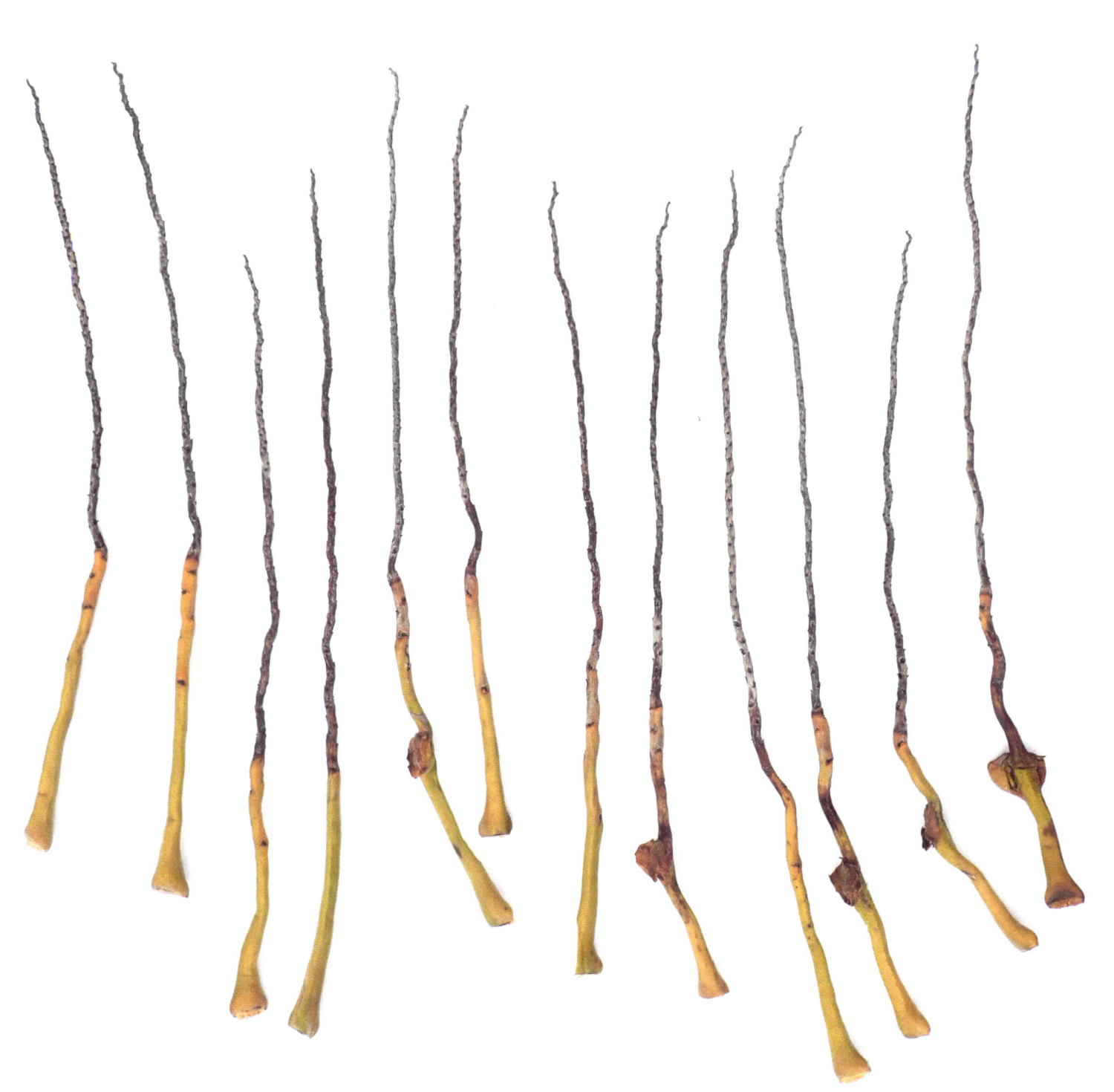

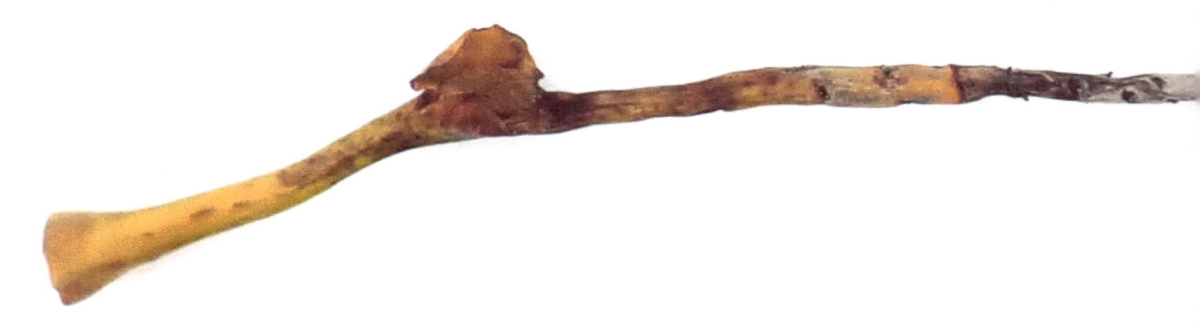

38   *Coconut Stems* (detail)

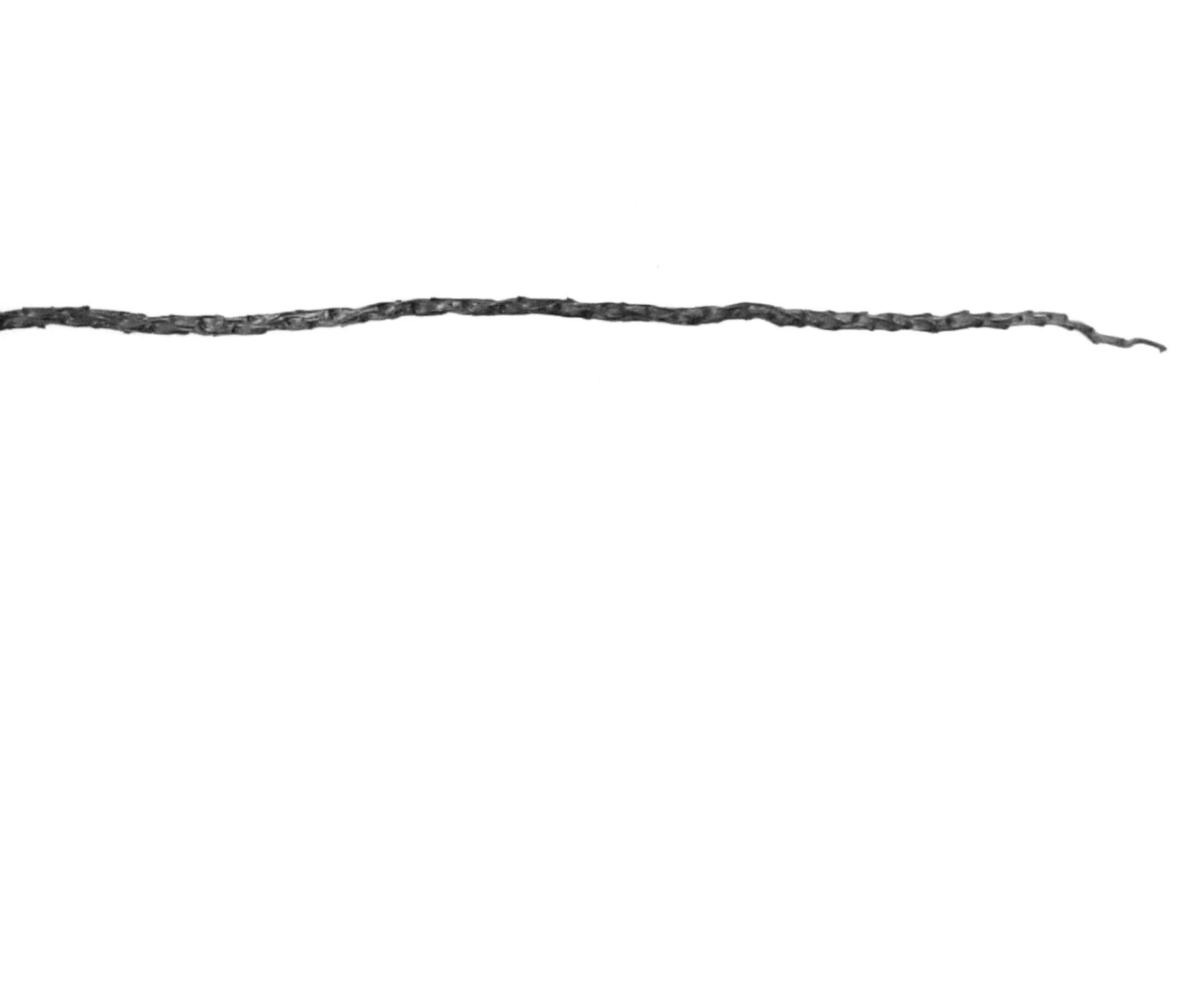

TURTLE ISLAND

At night a gold-throated
anole climbs the walls
inside our house
while outside it's rats,
all the way down.

They bite holes
in the screens,
infiltrate the attic,
their noises enter
your dreams.

Emptying our traps
over the edge of the dock –
for a minute they
seem to come to life
swimming for the shore,
brown fur fluffing
out, in the turquoise water.

Callyspongia Vaginalis   30 × 30 inches, archival pigment print, 2017

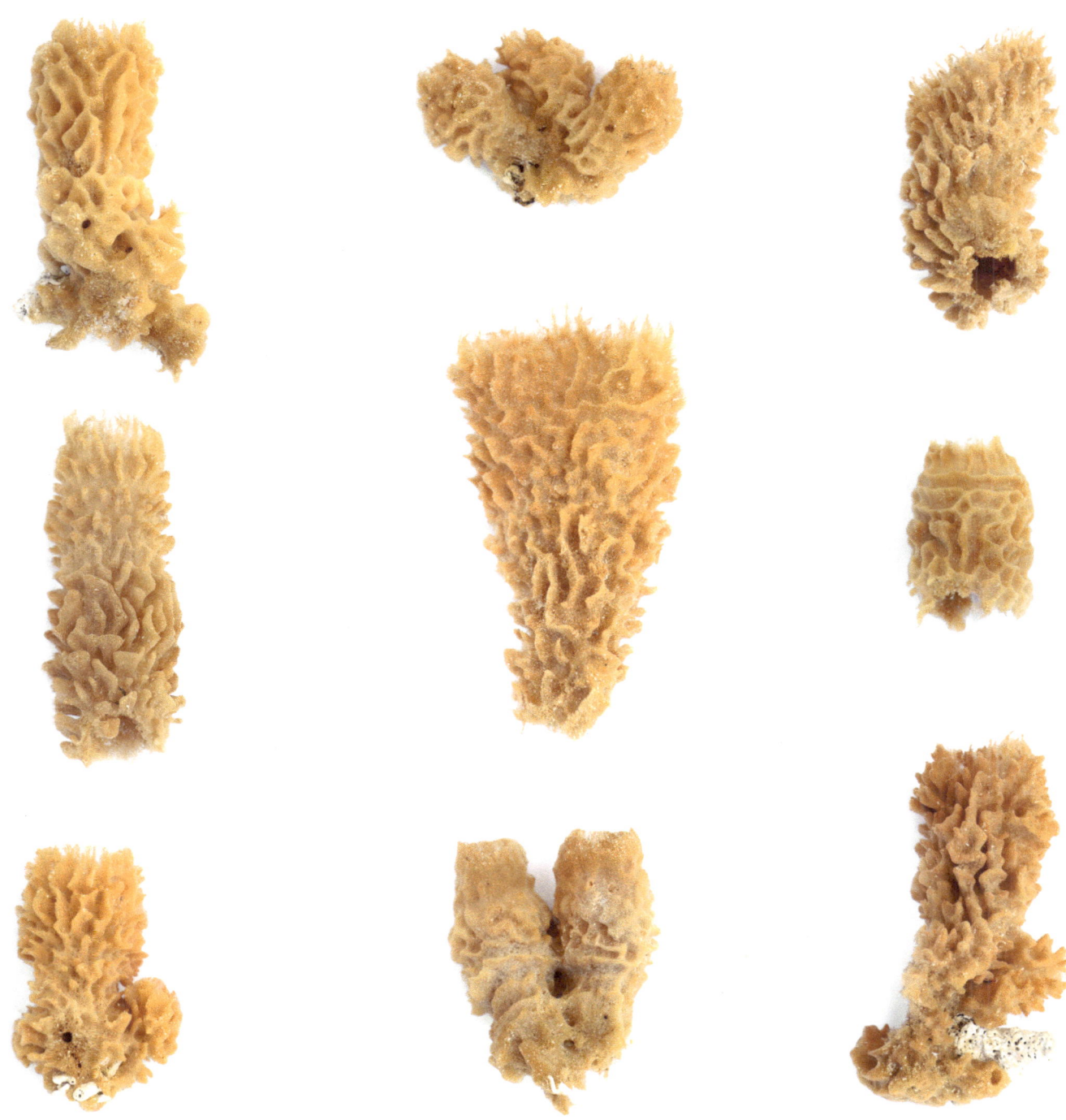

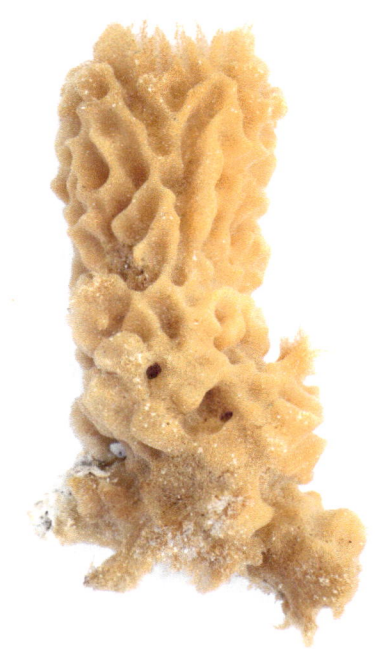

44   *Callyspongia Vaginalis* (detail)

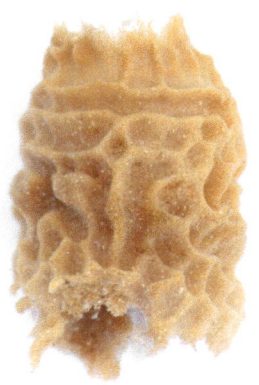

Callyspongia Vaginalis (detail) 45

THINKING LIKE OUR ISLAND

Did it wonder as I did if
it made the right decision
when it hunkered down to
wait out the hurricane?

Did it think this
purple sky is really extra-
ordinary,
those winds, that rain.

Where is everyone?

I could be crushed by
a falling thing,
no matter all I've done
to be ready.

And when the morning
came shining,
still, was that
something,
nothing, or just
another thing, among
the myriad things?
It was something –

I did not know
my pockets could fill with
so much water.

When we returned
did it think
there they are again
with their bony feet
what odd birds
so much gobble-gobble and
walking in circles.

Or wonder
how much longer
must I carry such weight?

Coconuts   30 × 30 inches, archival pigment print, 2017

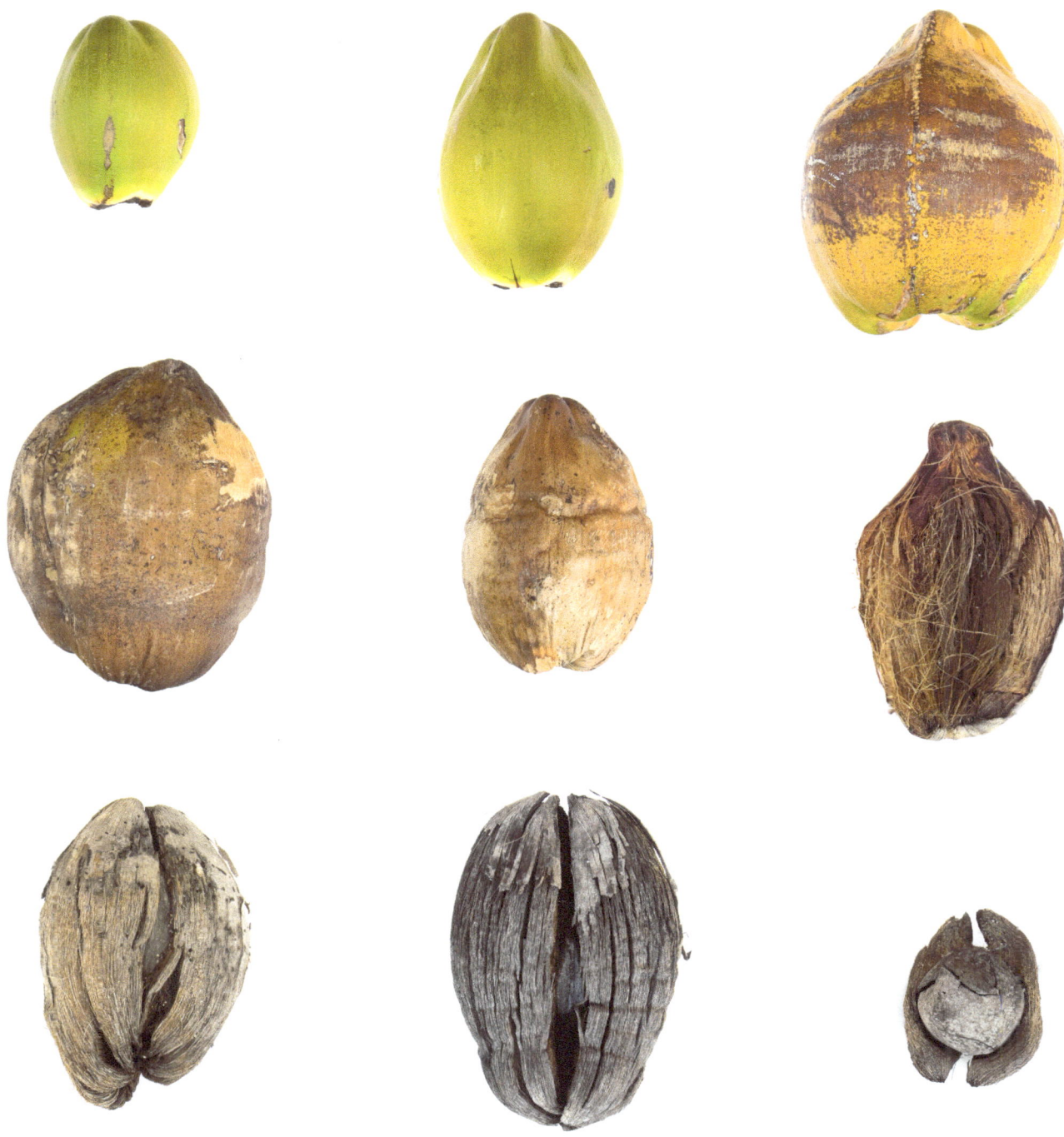

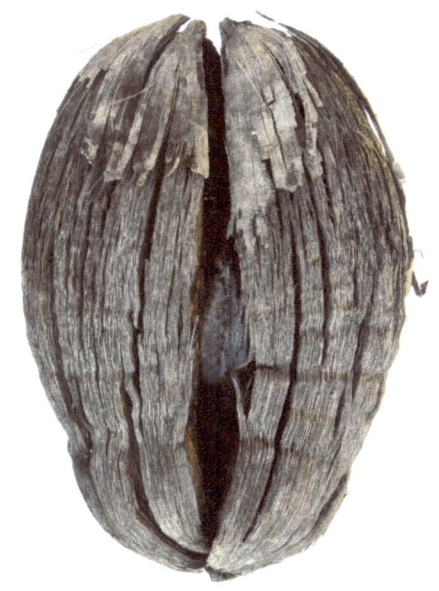

50   *Coconuts* (detail)

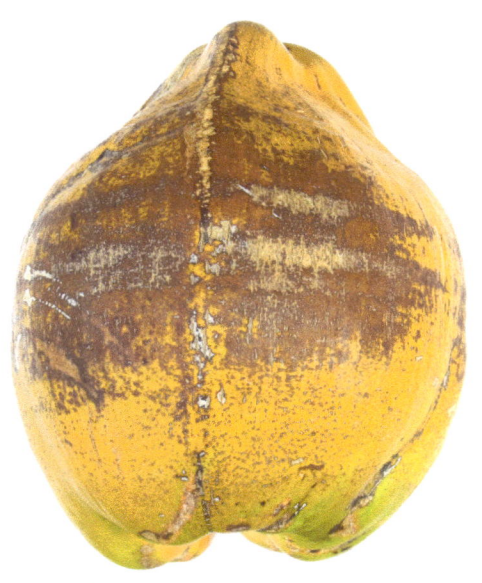

LOGGERHEAD KEY ON RETURN, AFTER IRMA

The air was not close after the storm, indeed, the sky tumbled brightly with fresh cumulous.

Palms, straightened already at the crown, had resumed their breezy whispering but not yet pulled up roots, or begun falling, after all, to ground with their young. Coconuts were everywhere, and long fronds, heavy at the shoulder, leaf tips soured rufous from sea blast, fanned out in the grass, which had been taken over by crow's feet and some other weed, like a goat head, with a nasty prick.

Hard buttonwood branches, snapped at odd angles, had scattered their salt-scorched leaves. Tight masses of spider lilies, with their green guard of nopales, were still standing at attention, though their white blooms and golden pistils were long gone, surrendered to the wind.

In the turquoise shallows, the corals were fanned, feathered, grooved, and star spangled, fingered and bulbous, fringed by multiple spongiforms and sheltering damsel fish, colors luminescent and pace slow, all as usual, not, as we'd feared, bleached, broken, or blanketed with sediment. The little fishes still swam in clouds blooming out ahead of the larger ones, forever hunters and runners, with a rippling field of clear water between them.

Were there more dead moon jellies? To our minds, this would be a bad auger, for always they, like cockroaches, algal slimes, and some lichen, hold out as survivors of the highest order.

The whole island had shifted at shore and tip, the wind and tide had changed its shape and size, kicking up three or four feet of sand on one side, sucking away the same from the other. With the beaches so radically reformed, the end appeared to come early this season for the turtle eggs just warming or starting to pip. Even the great nests so lovingly labored over by the enormous turtle mothers were mostly washed out, along with the tracks they left, as they tractored up from the sea, seeking night's cool cover for their work.

Lilies at the shoreline had fared much worse and were lying long stemmed and limp, moist white bulbs entirely uprooted, their finely layered skin exposed and luminous in the first days after. A cormorant and a tern had crashed at opposite ends of the island, one black, one white, both appearing exhausted to their very bones, eyes still open. No scavengers had found them yet, and every feather was still in place, unruffled.

We'd gotten back around sunset, drank too much wine as we feasted on the dill & cucumbers we'd pickled and left in the fridge, which had kept running through the hurricane, and fallen asleep on top of the hot sheets. In our excitement to return, we'd forgotten the cabbages we'd carried with us up and down the peninsula as fellow runners among the tens of thousands fleeing the hurricane. Soon, we would set out the lentils, sunflower seeds and mung beans to start sprouting and see us through the next three weeks.

The morning dawned in unfamiliar silence. There were no birds. In the tidy world of the keeper's cottage we welcomed six fly people first, and named them in Park Service lingo: Alpha, Bravo, Charlie, Delta, Eagle, and Foxtrot. For a day or two, the eight of us seemed to be the only ones, then a cluster of dragonflies came around, Irma, Jose, Katia, Lee, and Maria, accompanied by a bite of midges, too small to make out.

Those early arrivals seemed to draw a hover of bright cheeked kestrels, who we first mistook for parrots, followed soon after by the rest of the *Falco* family, a merlin and four peregrines, a cast. The swallows and warblers were quick to return, along with the brown pelicans, royal terns, ruddy turnstones, boobies and noddies, the ill-fated cattle egrets, and the magnificent frigates. A single osprey settled at the top of the lighthouse, and for a day or two would sail out from his command, hunting, solitary, most likely, for the first time since his nest had fledged, talons stretched out, across the sea. Over the next three weeks the sky, shore and scrubland opened up and became home and haven to continuously arriving winged friends – great and little, common, threatened, and endangered, migrant and resident, adult and juvenile – indeed, some of the young of those who nest exclusively in the Dry Tortugas learned to soar and dip and hunt, all before our very eyes.

The native sea lavenders and bay cedars had suffered on all sides of the island, upturned, needles burned by sea salt and wind, and branches blackened, but inland they showed barely a trace of storm damage and, soon, even the most decimated who had not been carried off by the tides were showing tenacious signs of new growth. Colonies of inkberry were bronzed and necrotic, yet, in days, were sending up jade-tipped, translucent shoots through the white sand. The two huge sea grape trees had their thick, round leaves toasted russet on the windward sides, but were green and thriving on their lees, with tiny pink veined infants leafing out within a couple of weeks.

We found the yellow-bellied writing spider who lives in the heart of the island entirely unperturbed. She was head down in hunting position, still and perfectly framed by her stabilimentum, a thick-woven lattice cross traversing the center of her web, which, reportedly, she feasts upon nightly and rebuilds every new day, writing and rewriting. Whether she had consumed him while mating, or he was late to return, there was no male in evidence. She didn't move and we detoured around only to stumble into another web that stuck to our bodies and trailed behind us for the next hundred yards until we managed to disentangle ourselves.

A turtle hatchling burst out of the sand at our feet during our sunset walk on our last evening, followed by a large ghost crab, pulling him back to certain death. Quick as we could, we dug them both out and, crab fleeing sideways, we sheltered the tiny newborn until the moon rose. When we released him to the ocean he made his way quickly, leaving only the tiniest tracks in the luminescent sand. He was bound, we knew, for his "lost years" where he would, god/dess willing, nestle into the grassy meadows of the ocean bed to feed and grow for some poorly understood period of time. With luck, he will continue to evade predators and eventually become a young adult, pelagic, born for a life at sea.

58   *Sea Grape Leaves*   30 × 30 inches, archival pigment print, 2017

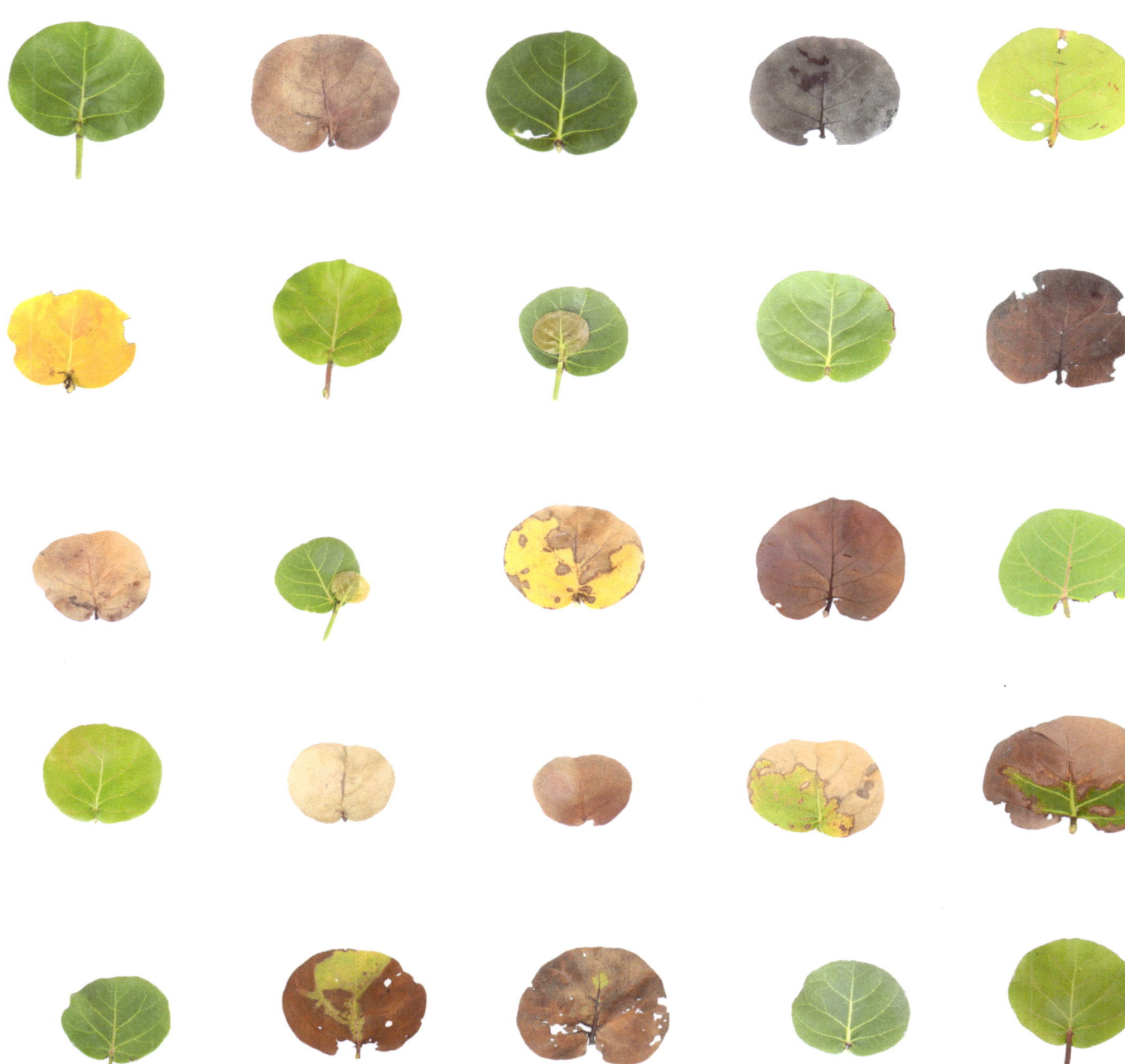

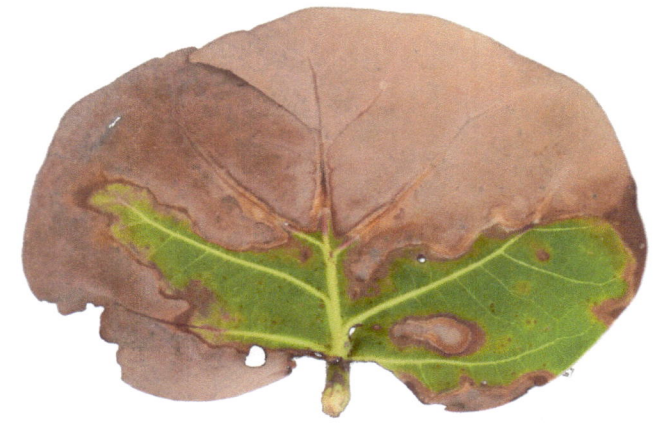

60   *Sea Grape Leaves* (detail)

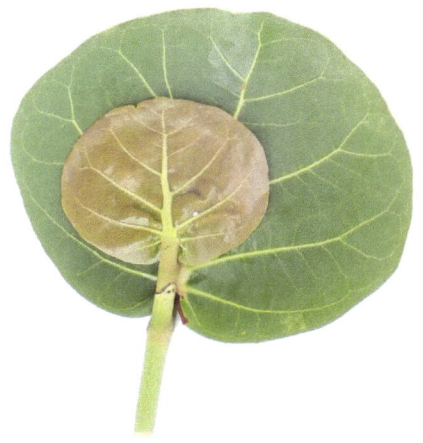

Sea Grape Leaves (detail)   61

ANIMAL VEGETABLE MINERAL

Trying to identify the
raptor in our field,
Matthew mentions
he is not a great fan of
Linnaeus. An explanation
ensues having to do with
classes or phyla or kingdoms.
Grasp weak on such things,
my mind wandered,
a blue-winged thing dropped
from the sky, hovered
over a yellow-bellied
winged thing whose
white eyebrows had
captivated me earlier
in the broad day –
twitching, I thought
with worry – and with
no apparent effort
snatched her (or him)
from the mid air just
as I realized I had not
been listening, or even
looking, just wondering
idly, whether the beans

might be done. Now
headed for the cottage,
our footsteps synchronize
even as we squabble
over whether the
intermittent wind is,
or is not,
a distant hurricane,
edgy with hunger.
Barely clothed,
I will dance
in the kitchen as he
prepares our meal, again
we will feast as gods
at rest after so much
christening, and fall
soundly to sleep only
when our skins cool and
the full moon sinks
at last into the sea.
High on their perch, cheeky
kestrels observe our every
move, tails bobbing.
Soon, it will be they
who know our names.

Gorgonians   30 × 30 inches, archival pigment print, 2017

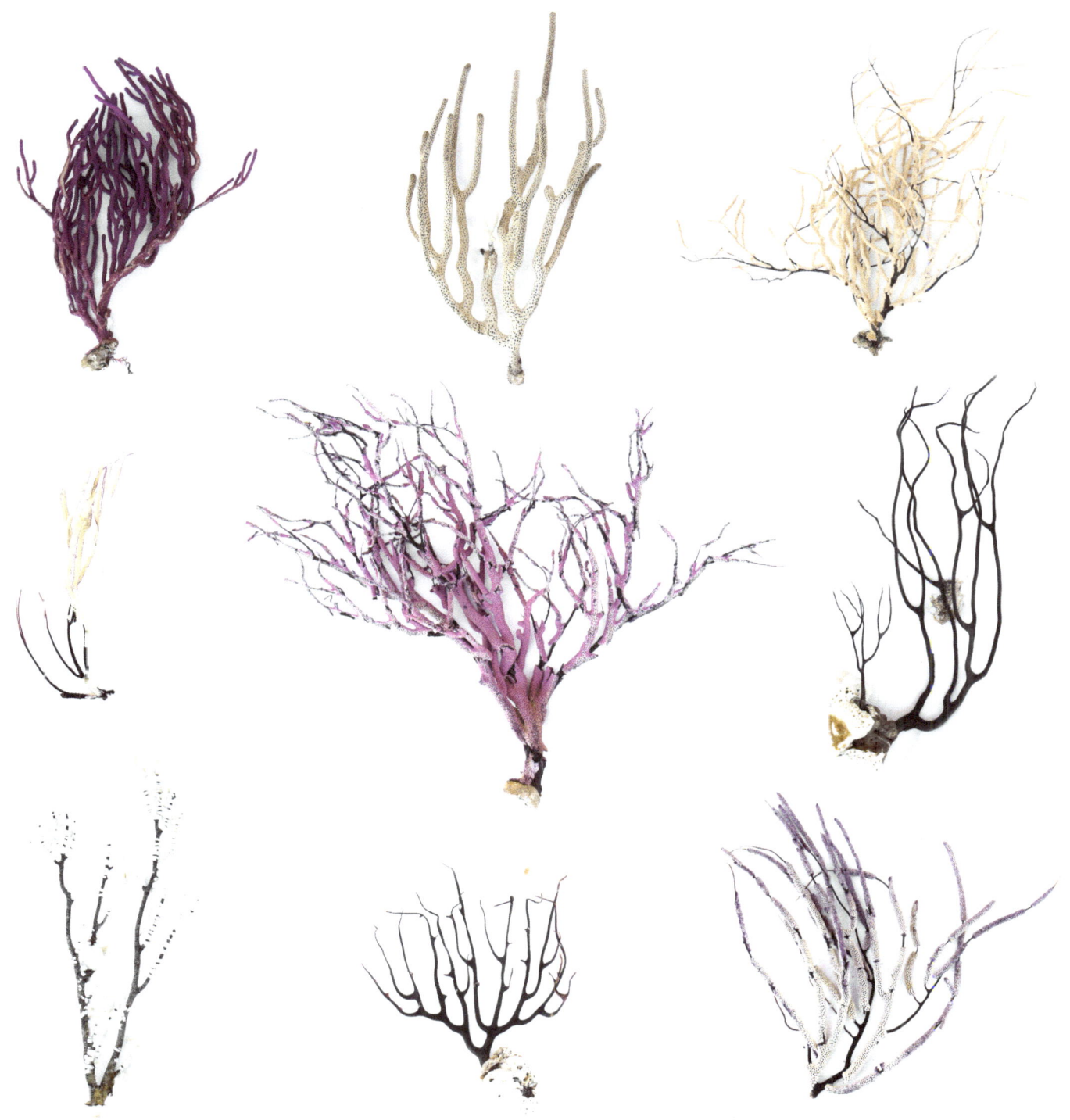

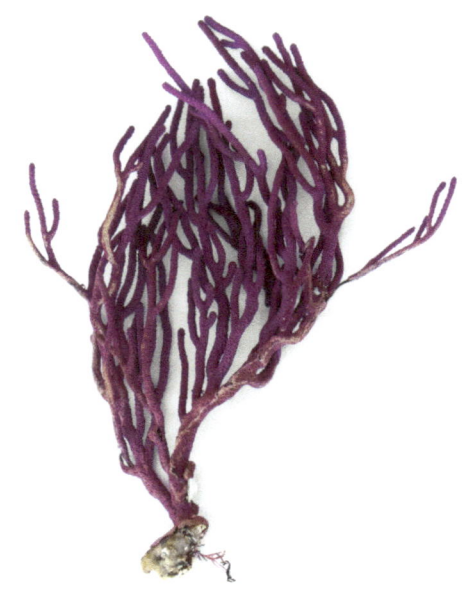

66   *Gorgonians* (detail)

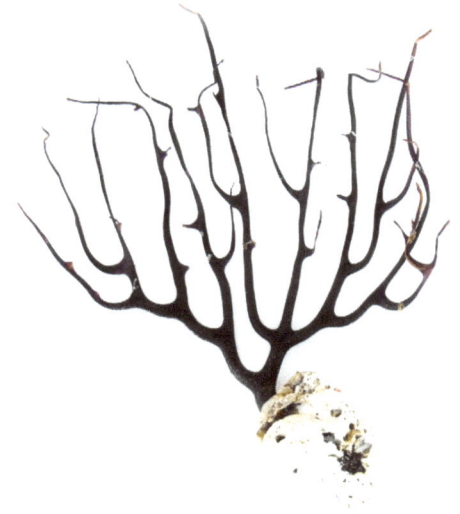

Gorgonians (detail)   67

RAISING FOOD IN THE TROPICS

My sunflower sprouts cannot lift their heads and
the lentils have mold growing at their feet. Crestfallen
I scrape the withered little radicles into the
compost barrel, wishing them well as future soil
warming in the sun, which has gone missing
for now, overthrown by the sky.

Suddenly ferocious again, the wind and sea have
swept away our coastline amble,
along with the royal terns at the dock, where,
recently confused by Hurricane Irma, six
gold-crowned cattle egrets had assembled,
unaware they'd begun starving on landfall.

Hopeful still, they circle and circle
searching out the necessary beast,
while, one by one, peregrines
cut them out of the sky.
We found three carcasses today, picked
clean to the bloody spine.

This week, Matthew's own back seizing,
we orbit the house tightly where
the ice packs are, and the bed,
where we fall in the heat, unabated.

Coming in waves, the far-reaching edge of a
new hurricane has gradually converged with
the full moon at perigee and, now, apparently,
a king tide is rising, astronomical.

Rising and rising, it takes out a mooring,
overcomes the dock, and inundates the
lagoon that had only just formed and become a
bathing ground for migrant shore birds.

Fracturing into rain, it surges, the
whole house perspires, beading up
the doors and windows swell,
our pores achieve a state of
continuous ejaculation, glands working
day and night like rain spouts,
cataracts, gushing sweat only to
meet deluge, spilling out to meet spray,
meet cloud, fog, mist, vapor.

Mowing the lawn in the penumbral light
between downpours, I raise up a pasture of
insects, momentary stock and savior for a
lone egret, who, presently, as the storm breaks
is strolling about, sovereign.

70   *Calcareous Halimeda Algae*   30 × 30 inches, archival pigment print, 2017

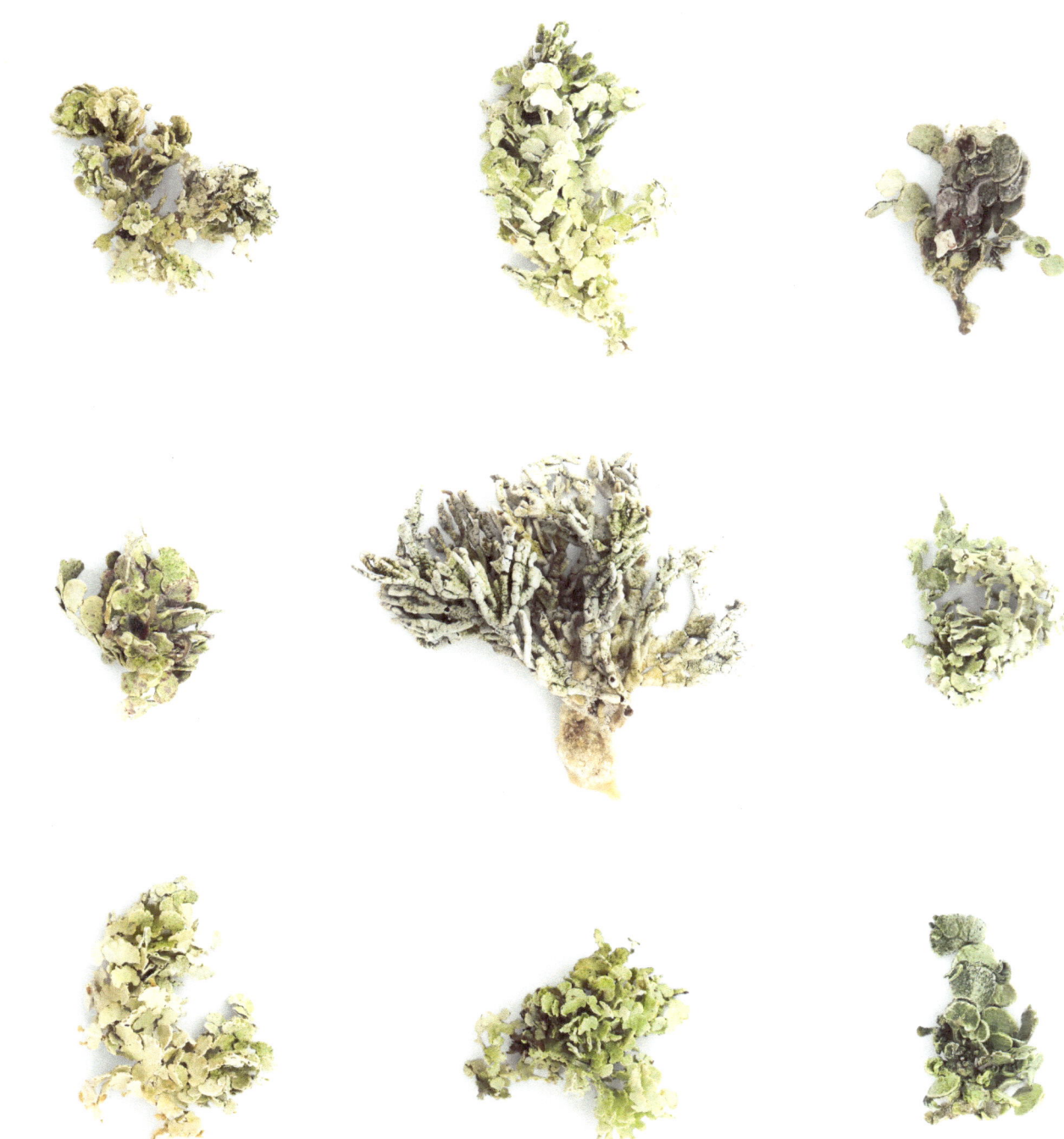

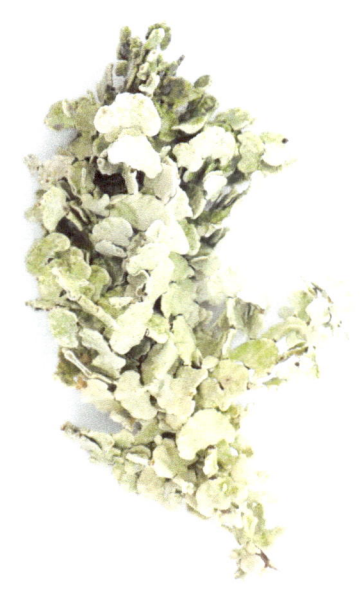

Calcareous Halimeda Algae (detail)

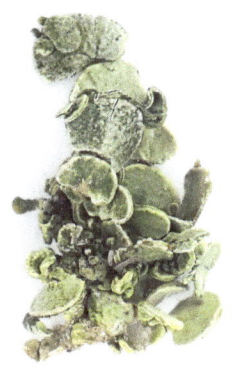

Calcareous Halimeda Algae (detail)   73

OCTOBER SQUALLS

Gusty squalls of wind shriek through the windows, which can't quite close for days now. Intermittent downpours of rain come sideways from the north and pelt the glass. Dawn breaks slowly. Clouds hang to the east and the rosy light is blocked. The hurricane washed out some of the lilies along the west shoreline and we found an unopened bottle of rum jammed upside down in one battered clump. Had the bottle floated across the sea and come to rest there, or was it the secret stash of a lighthouse keeper or a coast guard employee whose washed-out trash middens dot the shore nearby? That trash is now being pulled out of the burn pits by the high tide each day and hundreds of fragments of glass lie scattered down the beach. We collect many and pile them on the disused cistern near the cottage that serves as a staging area for the photography studio. Still half-buried in the piles are bundles of crumpled sheet copper, oxidized green by the salt and heat, and rusted conglomerations of steel bolts. Later in the morning the sun peeks out, but a moment later the rains start again, tapping on the glass and darkening the room.

Our days are measured by ambles along the beach. We time these with the tides, our moods, the heat of the sun, and the bouts of rain. Each walk shows us new details washed in or out by the weather and the tides. Loggerhead Key feels temporary, transitory. The isolation here is not cultural. It's fundamental, geological. We've lived mostly in the mountains, along colliding tectonic plates and the geological uplifts and folds of the Adirondacks, the San Gabriels along California's San Andreas Fault, in Santa Fe's Sangre de Cristos. The geology is nothing like that here. Loggerhead Key is a fugitive bar of sand, barely rising above the high tide. A hole dug a few inches deep anywhere reveals the same white coral and shell sand that our bare feet churn through on our daily circumambulations on the beach. And were we to dig deeper? More sand and coral rubble and perhaps limestone, which is made of more of the same. This land wasn't made by an expulsion of molten lava from the earth's fiery core. It wasn't made through the collision of continents. It was made, is being made and unmade every day, slowly, wistfully, by wave and tide and current, layering one grain of sand upon another.

This island is like a ship upon these waters, with no mountain, no stone, no fixed position, save for the buildings placed here over the past 165 years. These buildings cannot move with the shifting topography, and while the tall lighthouse still stands erect in the island's center, the foundations of the Carnegie research station that once dominated the northwest shore have largely crumbled back into the sea at the eroding coastline. Nearby, a boathouse once had a long dock extending out to the west from the shore. That was pulled apart long ago. Last March, the concrete-walled boathouse itself was undermined by waves and snapped in half with a sound like an earthquake. One end remains intact, perched above the beach. The other end is tilted strongly down into the sea itself. The high tide washes fresh sand in and out. The hurricane just took what was left of the heavy concrete floor. As extreme weather increases and sea levels rise, it appears that the remnant walls and roof will soon topple into the sea.

Weathered Conch Shells   30 × 30 inches, archival pigment print, 2017

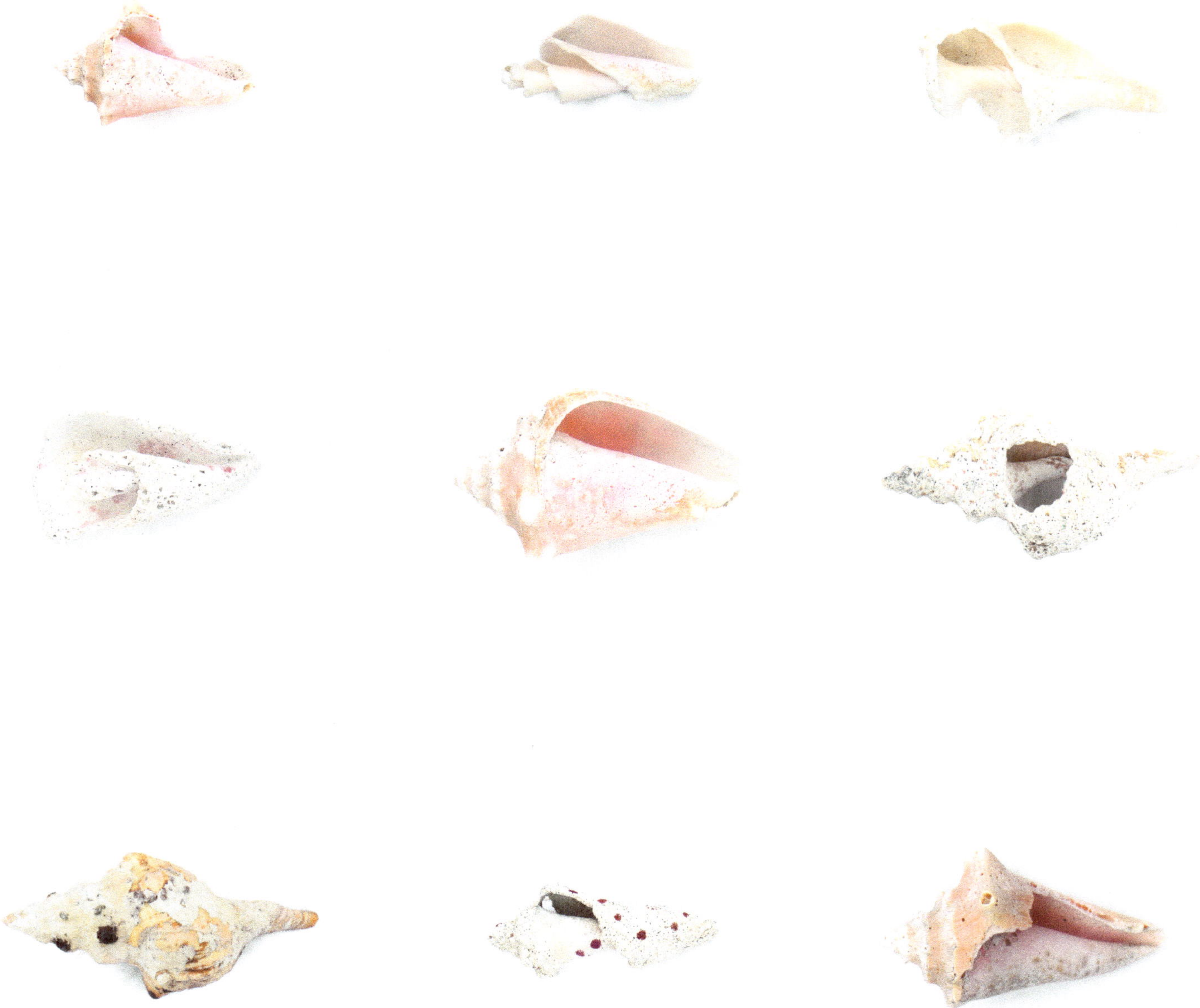

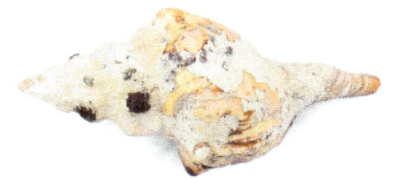
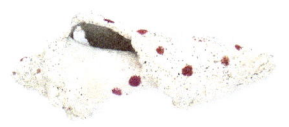
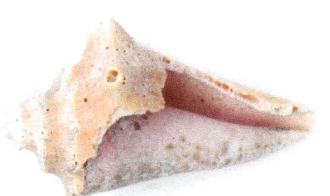

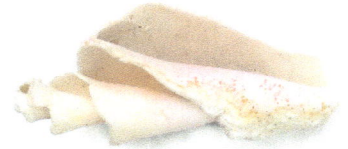

78   *Weathered Conch Shells* (detail)

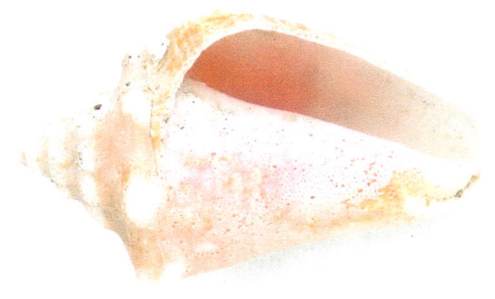

Weathered Conch Shells (detail) 79

NATURE LOVES A MIMIC

We venture out with the
incipient light between
weather surges, rounding
and rounding the island,
each to his own work,
and grooming
the grounds into a
fresh state of pristine
sanctuary. I come to see
Loggerhead Key
as a beautifully cultivated
mimic of nature, drawing
visitors like pollinators
who might, dallying here
and sailing home,
just be the very ones
who save it,
the virginal reef,
and, incidentally,
our plundered world,
as they go about
doing the great work,
knowingly or not,
of virtuous dissemination.

Sea Biscuits and Red Heart Sea Urchins 30 × 30 inches, archival pigment print, 2017

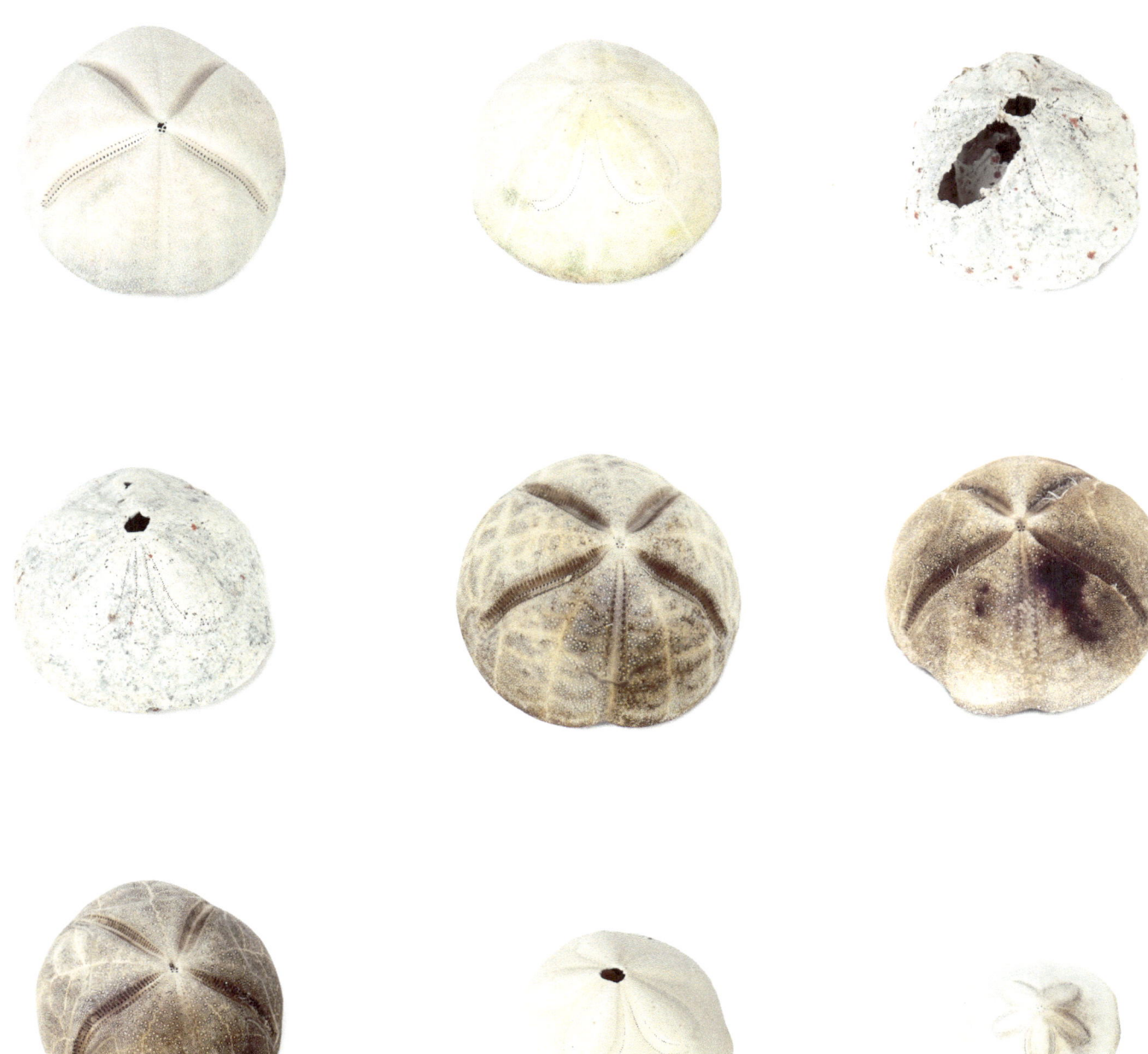

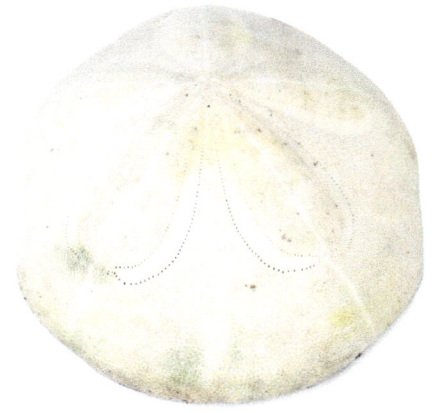

84   *Sea Biscuits and Red Heart Sea Urchins* (detail)

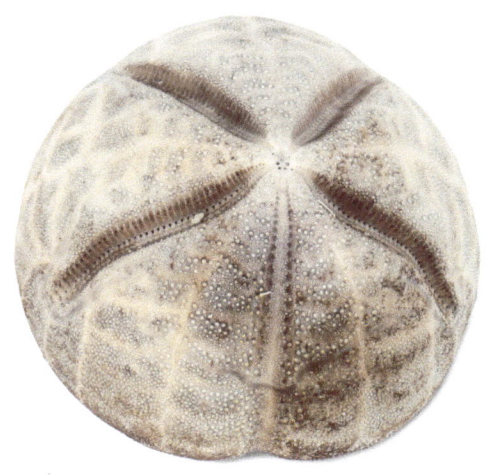

ON RETURNING HOME

He sees a hawk
the first morning, as he
heads to town, and I
a raven, later,
both of us late risers
fond of our nests.
The dawn
had been nearly
violent in its reds and
yellows as we explored
the familiar sheets,
reviewed the territory of
our bed.
A magpie, flashing
black and white,
followed my afternoon
path with the dog,
arroyo washed hard
by rain, clouds long gone,
air so thin
we could all
slip through it.
Maybe it was just
passing through
as wind does here,

in the high desert,
no clinging
scent of chamisa
at the end of the season,
the beginning of fall.
Animals, all, buoyant
today: we breathe
in, home as
joyous enterprise
and out, as open gate.

Hermit Crabs, Walking   30 × 30 inches, archival pigment print, 2017

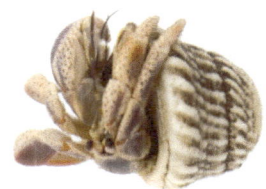
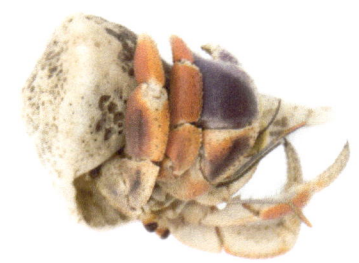
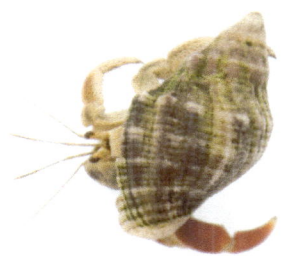
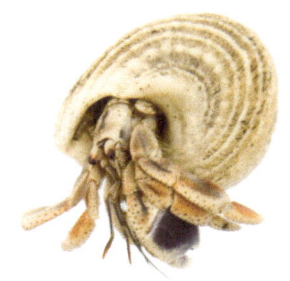
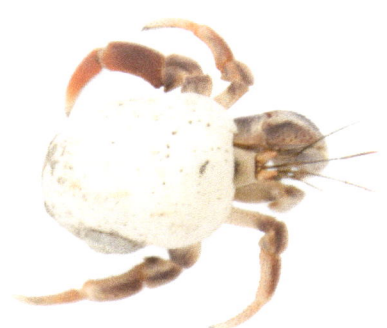
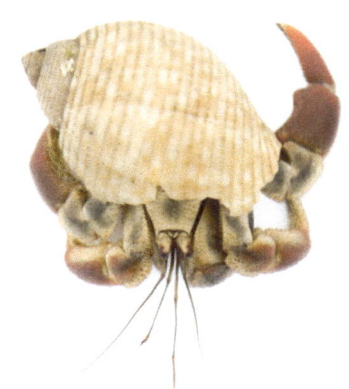
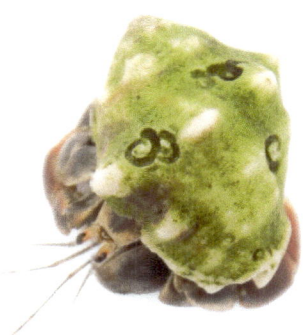
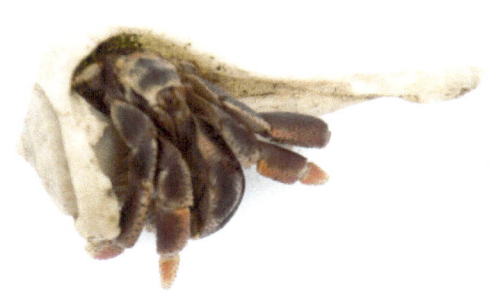
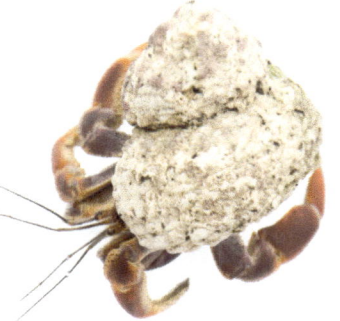

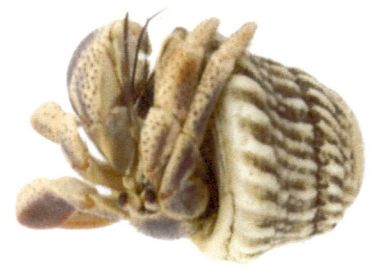

90   *Hermit Crabs, Walking* (detail)

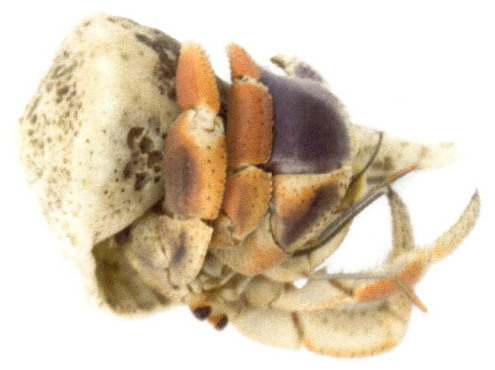

Hermit Crabs, Walking (detail)　91

BIBLIOLOGY
Readings from before and during our time on the island.

A Brief History of Seven Killings: A Novel
Marlon James, 2015

American Primitive
Mary Oliver, 1983

America's Fortress:
A History of Fort Jefferson, Dry Tortugas, Florida
Thomas Reid, 2006

Art Forms in Nature
Ernst Haeckel, 1904

At the Dry Tortugas During the War
Emily Holder, 1892

Beachcomber's Guide to Gulf Coast Marine Life
N. Fotheringham, S. Rothschild, P. Menefee, 1980 & 1989

Desert Islands and Other Texts 1953-1974
Gilles Deleuze, 2002

Devotions upon Emergent Occasions
John Donne, 1624

Dry Tortugas National Park
Submerged Cultural Resources Assessment
Ed. Larry E. Murphy, 1993

Encyclopedia of Coastal Science
Ed. Maurice Schwartz, 2005

Facing Gaia: Eight Lectures on the New Climatic Regime
Bruno Latour, 2017

FEMA Independent Study Courses
100   Introduction to Incident Command System
200   ICS For Single Resources and Initial Action Incident
700   National Incident Management System: An Introduction
800   National Response Framework: An Introduction

Feral: Rewilding the Land, the Sea, and Human Life
George Monbiot, 2017

Florida's Birds: A Handbook and Reference
Herbert W. Kale II, David S. Maehr, 1990

For Love of Matter: A Contemporary Panpsychism
Freya Mathews, 2003

Grzimek's Animal Life Encyclopedia
Vol. 3 Insects – Bernhard Grzimek, 2004
Vols. 4 & 5 Fishes 1 & 2 – Neil Schlager, 2003
Vol. 7 Reptiles – Michael Hutchins, 2003
Vols. 8 & 11, Birds 1 & 4 – Jerome A. Jackson, 2003
Vol. 9 & 10 Birds 2 & 3 – Bernhard Grzimek, 2003

Half-Earth: Our Planet's Fight for Life
E.O. Wilson, 2016

H is for Hawk
Helen Macdonald, 2014

Harper's New Monthly Magazine
Wrecking On The Florida Keys, 1859
The Dry Tortugas, Dr. J.B. Holden, 1868
Along the Florida Reef, Dr. J.B. Holden, 1871

Island Beneath the Sea: A Novel
Isabel Allende, 2011

Jack Tier: Or, The Florida Reef
James Fenimore Cooper, 1848

*Last Train to Paradise: Henry Flagler and the Spectacular Rise
and Fall of the Railroad that Crossed an Ocean*
Les Standiford, 2003

Morphic Resonance: The Nature of Formative Causation
Rupert Sheldrake, 1981

On the Origin of Species by Means of Natural Selection
Charles Darwin, 1860

Outside: Six Short Stories
Barry Lopez, 2014

Radial Symmetry
Katherine Larson, 2011

*Ranger Confidential:
Living, Working, And Dying in the National Parks*
Andrea Lankford, 2010

Regarding Wave
Gary Snyder, 1970

Sea Change: A Message of the Oceans
Sylvia A. Earle, 1996

*Seafaring Scientist:
Alfred Goldsborough Mayor, Pioneer in Marine Biology*
Lester D. Stephens, Dale R. Calder, 2016

Staying with the Trouble: Making Kin in the Chthulucene
Donna Haraway, 2016

The Art of Stillness: Adventures in Going Nowhere
Pico Iyer, 2014

The Caribbean before Columbus
W.F. Keegan, C.L. Hofman, 2017

The Etiquette of Freedom
Gary Snyder and Jim Harrison, 2010

The Loggerhead Turtle in the Eastern Gulf of Mexico
Charles R. Lebuff Jr., 1990

The Life of Dr. Samuel A. Mudd:
Containing His Letters from Fort Jefferson, Dry Tortugas Island,
Where He Was Imprisoned Four Years for Alleged Complicity in the
Assassination of Abraham Lincoln
Nettie Mudd, 1906

The Ocean of Life: The Fate of Man and the Sea
Callum Roberts, 2012

The Reef Set: Reef Fish, Reef Creatures and Reef Coral (3 Volumes)
Paul Humann, Ned Deloach, 2013

The Sibley Field Guide to Birds of Eastern North America
David Allen Sibley, 2003

The Sixth Extinction: An Unnatural History
Elizabeth Kolbert, 2015

The Stokes Essential Pocket Guide to the Birds of North America
Donald and Lillian Stokes, 2014

The Theory of Island Bio-Geography
Robert H. MacArthur, 2001

The Tree Where Man Was Born
Peter Matthiessen, 1972

This Present Moment: New Poems
Gary Snyder, 2016

To Have and Have Not
Ernest Hemingway, 1944

What the Robin Knows:
How Birds Reveal the Secrets of the Natural World
Jon Young, 2013

ACKNOWLEDGMENTS

We extend our deep gratitude to the many people and organizations who helped make our artist residency possible as it morphed from a quiet month on Loggerhead Key to a whirlwind that widened to include evacuation, shelter, return, and island restoration.

The National Parks Arts Foundation as a whole, and founder-director Tanya Ortega and board member Kate Russell have been unwavering in their commitment and overflowing in their enthusiasm for our project. Their consistent embrace of the artists they support is a true gift, and the opportunities NPAF provides is of great value for the artists, the National Parks, and the wider community that is reached through the projects produced under their programs.

The Dry Tortugas National Park is a rare gem and we are privileged to have been given the opportunity to experience it in great intimacy. Park Manager Glenn Simpson shared his wealth of knowledge of the history and ecology of this amazing sanctuary and graciously included us in the daily logistical updates with park staff and interns during and after Hurricane Irma. He saw the value of having us return to the island as soon as possible after the hurricane, and was dedicated to making that possible. Tree Gottshall, having lived and worked on Garden Key longer than he cares to remember, has both a strong connection to the place and a deep knowledge of the systems, mechanical and ecological, that sustain it. He shared this with us and trusted us to care about, to understand, and to work to maintain Loggerhead Key while we were there. DRTO Law Enforcement officer Karl Hildebrand calmly made sure we were safe as the hurricane approached, and helped arrange the logistics of our evacuation and safe shelter in Lady Lake.

The National Park Service's Volunteers in the Parks Program, through which this arts residency is possible, is a valuable exchange that helps to maintain and promote the beauty and wealth that is contained in these natural and cultural sites across the country. Yung Jones, the intern who was responsible for monitoring the turtle nests on the island while we were there, is a skilled and enthusiastic educator, who shared her abundant knowledge and great passion for the coral reef and all its creatures great and small. All the NPS staff were a pleasure to meet, helpful and generous with their stories and enthusiasm, including the crew of the ship NPS Fort Jefferson, Tim, Mikey, and Bryan, and the post-Irma sawyer crew led by Lucas Flickinger. It was an honor for us to serve with them during the recovery efforts and through our work here.

Our friends Elizabeth Jacobson and David Kaufman unhesitatingly gave us the keys to their apartment in Miami Beach, where we stayed for a week after the storm. The owners, managers, and staff of the Holiday Inn Express in Lady Lake worked tirelessly, with and without electricity, during and after Hurricane Irma, making sure that all – including family dogs – were welcome and safe as the hotel swelled to capacity with people fleeing from more dangerous areas in South Florida.

We offer our tremendous thanks to our donors – everyone who contributed to the fundraising campaign launched by NPAF to cover the unexpected expenses of our evacuation. That financial assistance made it possible to remain in Florida safely, to stay focused on our mission of observation and interpretation, and to be poised to return to the island to aid in the recovery there. The outpouring of care and concern from family and friends was a moving reminder that our relationships have deep power and lasting impact. We were very fortunate, indeed, to take shelter amid such blessings.

Healing in all the areas that were devastated by Irma remains ongoing, even at this writing. We witnessed the damage throughout the keys as we made our way back to the island, and follow closely the news from Puerto Rico, and throughout the Caribbean, where Hurricane Maria followed soon after. Our hearts travel with the survivors as they navigate life in a world turned upside down by the hurricanes of 2017.

Many thanks to our editors and readers for this book, Michael and Melody of Burning Books, Elizabeth Jacobson, Karen Chase, and Michele Daniel.

New images of Loggerhead Key are still arising in our dreams, conversations, and creative work. Our deepest gratitude goes to the island, which was and will always be for us both sanctuary and storm.

Matthew & Julie, March 2018

CLAVIS AUREA
an index of sorts

Archelon
Sea Turtle
Carapace
Plastron
Bridge
Pelagic
Cosmopolitan

Circling Wind
Depression
Displacement
Surge
Still Eye
Hurricane

Swallow
Warbler
Merlin
Magnificent Frigate
Aerial
Peregrine

Refugee
Migrant
Colonizer
Native
Island
Equilibrium

Ultramarine
Tropical Sea
Cerulean
Mother of us all
Symbiotic Host

Jellyfish
Sea Anemone
Fan Coral
Soft Bodied
Homologues

Queen Conch
Muscle
Vagina
Roseate
Parallelism

THE AUTHORS

Matthew and Julie Chase-Daniel have been living talking, exploring, and working together since 1984, in New York, Paris, and since 1989, in Santa Fe, New Mexico. Their individual and collaborative projects include poetry, photography, sculpture, and their son, Aquila.

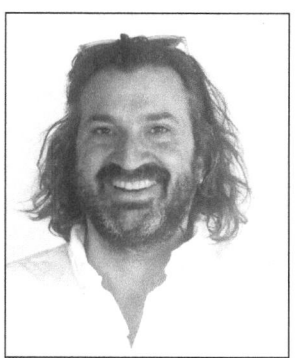 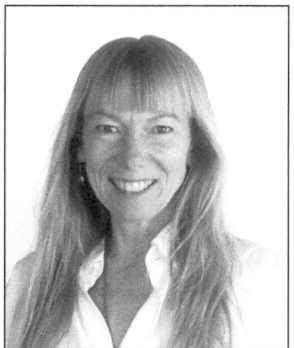

www.ingramcontent.com/pod-product-compliance
Lightning Source LLC
Chambersburg PA
CBHW050849180526
45159CB00007B/2626